Your Class as a Character Education Community

EDWARD F. DeRoche
DIANE D. JOHNSON

Copyright © 2024 Edward F. DeRoche, Diane D. Johnson
All rights reserved
First Edition

NEWMAN SPRINGS PUBLISHING
320 Broad Street
Red Bank, NJ 07701

First originally published by Newman Springs Publishing 2024

ISBN 979-8-89308-265-4 (Paperback)
ISBN 979-8-89308-267-8 (Hardcover)
ISBN 979-8-89308-266-1 (Digital)

Printed in the United States of America

Compromise starts with communication. Successful relationships require *communication.*

—Ed DeRoche

This book is dedicated to the professors, teachers, and administrators who, in our professional lives, took the time to befriend us, advise us, counsel us, warn us, tolerate us, and contributed to our love of teaching and administration (on the good days).

The book is also dedicated to the teachers, administrators, counselors, and parents who promote and foster character development at home, in school, and in their communities.

This book is dedicated to Danny Gene Johnson, Frank and Jacqueline Esposito, and Stephen Johnson for all your encouragement, love, and support. Also to the UNC Rex Cancer Center and health care team: Dr. Joellen Speca, Dr. Lim, Dr. David Eddleman, and Dr. Rebecca Cloer.

Contents

Acknowledgments vii
Planning—The Why? 1
Character Education—The What? 6
Character Education Teacher-Leader 13
The Model Standards Report 17
Character and School Climate..22
Character and Emotions...26
Social-Emotional Learning 31
Parents/Caregivers 35
The Arts 40
Service Learning...44
Relationships..48
Self-Discipline/Self-Management 51
Restorative Justice 56
Social Skills 61
Teaching Patience..67
Finding a Purpose..70
Setting Goals..77
Getting Motivated..80
Expectations...84
The Payoff..88
Our Q and A...91

Acknowledgments

Mary Williams (three books).
Michele Gallo, Nancy Girvin, and CJ Moloney.
Patricia McGinty and CJ Moloney Serena Pariser.

A special thanks to Serena Pariser for editing the manuscript and offering suggestions about the book's content and design. Serena is the bestselling author of *Real Talk About Classroom Management* and coauthor (with Ed DeRoche).

She is also author of these popular books for teachers and administrators:

Five to Thrive: Answers to Your Biggest Questions about Creating a Dynamic Classroom.

Real Talk about Classroom Management: 57 Best Practices That Work and Show You Believe in Your Students (2nd edition)

Answers to Your Biggest Questions about Creating a Dynamic Classroom

It Starts in the Classroom: Character Education Today for a Better Tomorrow

We also thank the manuscript editors, designers, production staff, and the publisher.

Edward F. DeRoche   Diane D. Johnson

Thank you to Sean and Hannah for all the guidance, editorial advice, and good constructive criticism on this book. We so appreciate all you have done to make this book a reality.

Planning—The Why?

Who is this "Classroom as a Character Education Community" book for?

Is it for *you*?

It is for beginning and veteran teachers, counselors, administrators, human resource specialist, and health care providers.

It is for undergraduate and graduate students in training to be teachers, counselors, and administrators looking for ideas and resources to *teach*, *model*, and *assess* character education initiatives in classrooms, schools, and the community. It is for parents and caregivers, community leaders, and volunteers who serve and educate children and youth.

We begin by looking at *the school site*.

The character development of students in our schools resides with the teachers, administrators, students, and parents in an individual school. That is, character initiatives are *school specific*.

Each school, even in the same school district, has its own unique cultural, economic, and social characteristics. Even where there is a district-wide character education program, each school puts its own spin on the program that best meets the needs of all students. Thus, we see each classroom as a *character education community* as one way to help you and others who want to know

- *why* and *when* to teach character;

- *what* to teach and *how* to do it;
- *what* resources will be needed;
- *how* to determine what works/what doesn't.

Organize now

Each school or school district should have a character educa-tion evaluation committee (CEEC). Membership on the committee should include teachers, administrators, counselors, classified per-sonnel, students, parents, and community representatives.

The point is that program evaluation work requires organiza-tion, leadership, and resources.

Committee members need to layout evaluation plans including setting a timetable of what needs to be assessed, when, and how.

"*You gotta know the territory*," so said the salesman in the musi-cal *The Music Man.*

"Knowing the territory" means that members of a school or district *Character Education Evaluation Committee* are educating themselves about character education practices, resources, research findings, and advice from the experts in the field. An important part in their role is taking the time to carefully review the data they have decides to seek—school culture reports, absentee rates, parents' expectations, student behavior reports, and the like.

Character Education Evaluating Committee members need to know about summative and formative evaluation. They need to develop the skills imbedded in asking questions.

Data-savvy committee

In our opinion, *question-asking* underscores the use of such eval-uation "tools" as testimonials, observations, focus groups, surveys, interviews, videos, case studies, and research reports.

Question-asking is the "camera" committee members will use for evaluating character education efforts.

Committee members and others can become "data-savvy" by following these four steps.

1. Identify questions that focus on factors to be evaluated.
2. Collect data that will answer these questions.
3. Study the data—what does it tell the committee.
4. Ask more questions, such as:

Did the Committee find any change in student behaviors?

Did the Committee find any changes in students' academic achievement?

Did the Committee find any need for "special intervention" programs?

Did the Committee find any data that suggest changes in teachers' instructional practices?

The benefits

We are often asked about the benefits of school-site evaluation efforts.

From what school personnel tell us there are many benefits.

We have selected four.

1. The process of evaluation contributes to the development of positive, collaborative relationships.
2. The process of evaluation strengths the "buy-in" to the mission, goals, and the need to teach students "character strengths."
3. The process brings stakeholders together to learn, practice, and apply evaluation techniques and strategies.
4. The process empowers school personnel, including students, to practice and value the methods for self-evaluation and self-reflection.

Commitment, purpose, and relationships

Let's discussed the why of planning, the need to organize, the importance of asking questions, the need for a "data-savvy" school committee, and the benefits of school-site evaluation efforts.

Our intent here is to encourage your students to think about, talk about, and practice CPR at home, at school, and in their classroom.

Commitments: The word *commitment* has several synonyms. We picked three—*intentionality, responsibility, and promise.* Two questions for classroom discussion might be: What can your students count on you to do? What promises should students make to you and their classmates?

Our job as educators (and parents) is to help students understand the importance of making and keeping commitments (responsibility/promises). This understanding will have a positive influence on their academic performance as well as their personal and social behaviors.

Purpose: "Our commitments give us a sense of purpose." (David Brooks, NYT journalist)

The question for you, for us, and other adults is: *How do we help students develop a sense of purpose about what they do in school, in classrooms, and elsewhere?*

How do we help children and youth learn to take responsibility for their actions, to be willing to accept the negative consequences of their actions and behaviors, be held accountable and be responsible to do something about them.

William Damon, Director of the Stanford Center on Adolescence, says a sense of purpose is "the long-term, number one motivator in life." He writes *(edited)*:

> *Schools must address the why question with students about all that they do. Why do people study math and science? Why is it important to read and write? To spell words correctly? Why have I (the*

*teacher) chosen teaching as my occupation? Why do
we have rules against cheating? Why are you, and
your fellow students, here at all?*

Relationships: It is the driver of change!

We need to pay more attention to "relationship factors" because strong relationships are the *"life lines"* in helping to reduce behavior issues, improve classroom climate, enhance student attitudes and attention, contribute to student achievement, and help reduce the negative effects of stress and boost one's self-esteem.

Your takeaways

Commitment, purpose, and relationships form your and your students' paths to a peaceful, promising, and productive school experience, the three capture essential behaviors that underscore the character formation of students.

Commitment, purpose, and relationships must be and can be *taught and modeled.*

Character Education—The What?

What is the *purpose* of education?

In their book, *Most Likely to Succeed* (Simon & Schuster, 2015, pp. 223–234), Tony Wagner and Ted Dintersmith write:

> *The foundation of all learning in the twenty-first century: co-knowledge, skill, and will.*
>
> *Of the three, we believe that will, or motivation is the most important… We are talking about the motivations that include grit, perseverance, and self-discipline, (and) the importance of the four C's: critical thinking, communication, collaboration, and creative problem-solving.*

Character education is the teaching and learning of moral and civic virtues, social and emotional skills, and character strengths such as kindness, gratitude, self-control, social skills, teamwork, diligence, perseverance, strong work ethic, positive attitudes, ingenuity, integrity, justice, caring, respect, and responsibility.

Educating for character helps students develop what they are passionate about; helps students develop creative problem solving skills and critical thinking skills; and prepares them to be knowledgeable and participating citizens.

Here are a few questions that you, your colleagues, and others in the community should talk about.

Why teach character at home and at school?

What character education programs should be taught—our own or others?

What are the cost factors for implementing a character education program?

How much training (professional development) will we need?

How do we seek and get "teacher buy-in"?

Who should take leadership responsibilities for developing and implementing the program?

Where will we find the resources and research?

What are the best strategies and methods for teaching "character strengths?"

How will we engage/involve students in efforts to develop their "character?"

How will we determine what works, what doesn't—and why?

We use the "umbrella" as a metaphor to answer the *what* question. The umbrella's "handle" is the center of a school's character education program, representing the strengths and virtues of educating for character.

Most umbrellas have eight panels. Each panel represents a component of a character education program. Vision, Mission, Goals, Objectives, Academic Programs and Standards Classroom Climate, and School Culture Curriculum Extracurricular Programs Assessment/ Evaluation Partnerships and Community-based Programs Special Programs, such as anger management, conflict resolution, social-emotional learning, empathy programs, drug and alcohol use/abuse, violence prevention, peace education, anti-bullying programs, student leadership programs, mindfulness strategies, and restorative justice practices.

To know more

Professor Thomas Lickona, suggests these *nine classroom strategies and three school-wide strategies* for an effective comprehensive approach to character education.

1. *The teacher as caregiver, model, and ethical mentor: treating students with love and respect, encouraging right behavior, and correcting wrongful actions.*
2. *A caring classroom community: training students to respect and care about each other.*
3. *Moral discipline: using rules and consequences to develop moral reasoning, self-control, and generalized respect for others.*
4. *A democratic classroom environment: using the class meeting to engage students in shared decision making and in taking responsibility for making the classroom the best it can be.*
5. *Teaching values through the curriculum: using the ethically rich content of academic subjects as vehicles for values teaching.*
6. *Cooperative learning: fostering students' ability to work with and appreciate others.*
7. *The "conscience of craft": developing students' sense of academic responsibility and the habit of doing their work well.*
8. *Ethical reflection: developing the cognitive side of character through reading, research, writing, and discussion.*
9. *Conflict resolution: teaching students how to solve conflicts.*
10. *Caring beyond the classroom: using role models to inspire altruistic behavior and providing opportunities for school and community service.*
11. *Creating a positive moral culture in the school: developing a caring school community that promotes the core values.*
12. *Parents and community as partners: helping parents and the whole community join the schools in a cooperative effort to build good character* (Thomas Lickona, PhD, Director, Center for the Fourth and Fifth Rs [Respect and Responsibility, *www.cortland.edu/character*]).

The Cs of character

There are only two *Cs* in the word *character*, but one can find many words that begin with *C* in describing good, positive character traits and behaviors. We compiled a few *C* words that show the attributes of character.

Caring

We thought that you might be interested in a way to assess how "caring" you are as a teacher.

So we created this ten-item caring factors scale.

Below are the ten "caring factors." If you want a "rating rubric" for each of the ten "habits," we included one example. It might be best to construct your own rubric.

____I do this well; ____I don't do enough of this; ____I need to work on this

1. I know each of my students' academic and social needs.
2. I have no problems giving my students a second chance.
3. I willingly talk to my students about their in-class and out-of-class problems.
4. I help my students set goals and offer advice regarding each goal on their list.
5. My students know that I care about them and will help them in any way I can.
6. I encourage my students to do the best that they can.
7. I'll go the "extra mile" for each of my students.
8. My students know and appreciate that I listen to what they say, even if they might be wrong.
9. I frequently ask each of my students for their opinions and their concerns.
10. I show genuine interest in my students because I know each of them as individuals.

Choice

Living a life of good character doesn't happen by *chance* nor does it happen by *circumstances*. It happens by *choices*.

> *It is our choices, Harry, that show what we truly are, far more than our abilities. What we make of ourselves, what we make of our lives, is a matter of choice—our choice and our responsibility* (Harry Potter counseled by the wise old headmaster, Dumbledore; paraphrased)

Citizenship

Two social studies specialists once wrote that the purpose of schooling is not to help people be better off but to be better scholars, citizens, and workers. They noted that a multicultural society needs "roots." These roots, they said, are described in our founding documents, in our symbols and slogans, and in our personal and public civic virtues. Our schools, therefore, are called to educate the young to uphold (and sometimes challenge) core virtues, such as trustworthiness, fairness, patriotism, justice, courage, responsibility, respect, and honesty.

Common sense

> *"Common sense" was preceded in death by his parents, Truth and Trust, by his wife, Discretion, by his daughter, Responsibility, and by his son, Reason. He is survived by his four stepbrothers.*
>
> *I Know My Rights*
> *I Want It Now!*

Someone Else Is to Blame
I Am a Victim.

—CS Obituary printed in the *London Times*, date and author unknown

Company

Character is how you behave in response to the company (peer groups, friends, family) you keep, seen and unseen.

—Psychologist Robert Coles, *The Call of Stories*, p. 198)

Who are the virtuous, the responsible agents, the moral teachers, and the positive role models that keep company with our young people? Is it their peer group, the entertainment industry, social media, Facebook, YouTube, the Internet?

Conscience

From the BC comic strip *Pearls of Wisdom*:

A conscience is what hurts when everything else feels great.

Mastroianni and Hart (July 2012)

No need for further comment.

Consequences

The penalty we pay or the internal–external rewards we receive from the choices we make. Behaviors have consequences, some positive, some negative. People make mistakes, including people of good character. But these people have what might be called "character strengths." They hold themselves accountable, take responsibility, pay the consequences, learn from their mistakes, and do not repeat them.

Courage

As we adults know, our courage is tested daily. The young can be taught to meet the personal and social challenges by having courage to do the right thing; to stand up for their own and other's rights, to make difficult decisions particularly when such decisions may not be easy or popular, and to have the courage to say "no" when "invited" to cheat, bully, harass, or be unfair, impolite, disrespectful to others.

What C words would you add to the list? Why?

Your message board

Questions/Thoughts/Ideas

Character Education Teacher-Leader

—John Maxwell

Let's talk about *you* and other teachers, counselors, and administrators as "character education leaders" in classrooms, schools, school districts, professional communities, and in the public arena.

Character educators are communicators, collaborators, consensus-builders, stand-bearers, researchers and evaluators who know about best practices. *Character educators* willingly share information about programs, curricular, instructional materials, special projects, student needs, parent initiatives, and evaluation efforts. *Character educators* favor partnerships that offer parents and caregivers opportunities to help meet students' physical, social, and emotional needs. *Character educators* value, understand, and use research to know what's working and not working and why. *Character educators* have a *vision* of what might/should be. They ask themselves: *who are we* (character and values), *how do we perform* (skills and talents), and *how shall we lead* (sharing, partnerships, team-building)?

To know more

The Teacher Leadership Competencies, published by the *National Board for Professional Teaching Standards,* notes that *teacher leaders shape the culture of their schools, improve student learning, and influence practice among their peers.*

They note that the competencies include:

> *Authoritative Leadership: push their teams to pursue common goals.*
> *Affiliative Leadership: are people who their teams can trust and feel safe going to.*
> *Democratic Leadership: are the first to seek feedback and share decision-making responsibilities.*
> *Pacesetting Leadership: focus on the practice of leading by example inside or outside the classroom.*
> *Coaching Leadership: mentor young or struggling teachers. (https://soeonline.american.edu/blog/teacher-leadership-roles)*

You should also know that Cindy Harrison *and* Joellen Killion published an article in the September 2007 issue of the ASCD that identified and describe these ten roles for teacher-leaders that help teachers contribute to their schools' success:

1. *Resource Provider.*
2. *Instructional Specialist*
3. *Curriculum Specialist*
4. *Classroom Supporter*
5. *Learning Facilitator*
6. *Mentor*
7. *School Leader*
8. *Data Coach*
9. *Catalyst for Change*
10. *Learner (https://www.ascd.org/el/articles/ten-roles-for-teacher-leaders)*

Your role

We hope that we are not being too repetitive when we remind you that *educating for character* means that your role as a *character educator-leader* is to

- demonstrate respect, care, and concern for the character development of your students and have them do the same for their classmates;
- create a positive learning environment;
- have positive relationships with your students, their parents, and with your colleagues;
- use character development activities that are engaging, positive, rewarding, and productive;
- communicate clearly with your students about being respectful and responsible;
- teach your students how to resolve conflicts;
- to listen to your students;
- make time for them;
- let them know care and trust them;
- show your students that you have a sense of humor;
- to make it clear to your students why you will do not tolerate disruptive behaviors;
- help your students admit their mistakes, learn from their mistakes, and, if necessary, offer apologies/restitution; and
- to share the information and resources in this book with your colleagues, parents, and others.

We end this chapter by asking you to consider these five standards that we hope will help you understand and appreciate your role as a character educator leader.

Standard 1: Instill a sense of responsibility, community involvement, and understand the democratic principles.
Standard 2: Foster empathy, kindness, and compassion towards others.

Standard 3: Develop well-rounded individuals who not only excel academically but also exhibit positive character traits in their interaction with others and in their contributions to society.

Standard 4: Promote the concept of fairness, justice and equality in all interactions and decision-making.

Standard 5: Hold your students accountable for their behaviors and decisions both academic and in a social context.

Standard 6: Encourage students to show respect for themselves and others including tolerance, appreciation, and diversity.

You may want to add additional standards here

Your message board

Questions/Thoughts/Ideas

The Model Standards Report

The "Model Standards Report" for the teaching and learning of character and social-emotional development *provides a roadmap for school leaders and teachers to help children and teens understand, care about, and consistently practice the SEL skills and character strengths that will enable them to flourish in school, in the workplace, and as citizens (https://www.character.org/model-standards).*

As a *character education leader* in your school and community, you are encouraged to read this report, reflect on it, discuss it with your colleagues and others, and use the ideas to develop your school's and/or district's character education and social-emotional programs and initiatives.

The *Model Standards* addresses the dimensions of four *character-strengths* and five skills of *social-emotional learning:*

Moral character;
Performance character;
Intellectual character; and
Civic character

Self-awareness, self-management, social awareness, interpersonal/ relationship skills, and responsible/ethical decision-making.

Section 4, Part 1 of the *Model* defines and describes the four character dimensions. Part 2 defines and describes the five skills of social-emotional learning. Each dimension is defined with outcomes by grade and age level, examples, and resources. An example: the skill of *self-awareness* for students in grades six to eight, ages eleven to thirteen.

There are *seven activities* to be learned and practiced. We selected three for this example.

Provide a roadmap for school leaders and teachers to help children and teens understand, care about, and consistently practice the SEL skills and character strengths that will enable them to flourish in school, in the workplace, and as citizens.

- *Describe how different thoughts, situations, and behaviors affect your feelings and emotions.*
- *Recognize the times when you exaggerate the severity or consequences of mistakes, embarrassing moments, failures, rejections and other negative events.*
- *List and explain the different external supports you have used when feeling stressed or anxious (e.g., family, friends, teachers, neighbors).*

In Section 5: Summary, the authors write:

> *The SEL skills help students consistently be honest and trustworthy, caring and compassionate, self-disciplined, intellectually curious, fair, and respectful.*
>
> *The CSED Model Standards provide school leaders with a unifying vehicle that will bring the staff together toward a shared goal and purpose: supporting students as they strive to become young people of character who will flourish in school, in relationships, in the workplace, and as citizens.*

To know more

Character.org also published this framework designed for school and community character education efforts. *Six core beliefs:*

1.   *The family is a child's first character educator.*
2.   *Character strengths and SEL skills are not add-ons, but rather add significant value to student success.*
3.   *A positive school climate is critical to fostering the whole child.*
4.   *Character and social-emotional development requires thinking, feeling, and doing (head, heart, and hands).*
5.   *The character strengths should be taught, caught, and sought.*
6.   *The Model Standards align with the full-range of classroom and school-based initiatives.*

Casel's Social-Emotional Framework—This framework connects five broad, interrelated areas of competence: self-awareness, self-management, social awareness, relationship skills, and responsible decision-making.

SEL is the process through which all young people and adults acquire and apply the knowledge, skills, and attitudes to develop healthy identities, manage emotions and achieve personal and collective goals, feel and show empathy for others, establish and maintain supportive relationships, and make responsible and caring decisions. (www.casel. org/what-is-SEL)

Program standards checklist

We created this checklist to help you and your colleagues determine the extent to which your school's character education efforts are in compliance with each of these statements using the numbers on this scale.

5 4 3 2 1
Compliance—Moderate Compliance—Noncompliance

Our school's character education program…

1. fosters and enhances the school's core virtues. 5 4 3 2 1
2. is guided by the school's mission and goals. 5 4 3 2 1
3. has a specific set of expectations and outcomes. 5 4 3 2 1
4. enables students to take leadership roles. 5 4 3 2 1
5. contributes to the moral and social development of all students. 5 4 3 2 1
6. is assessed on regular basis. 5 4 3 2 1
7. contributes to a positive school climate. 5 4 3 2 1
8. is integrated into the school's regular curriculum and its co-curricular programs. 5 4 3 2 1
9. values the multicultural traditions of students and their families. 5 4 3 2 1
10. provides teachers, staff, and students with the resources needed for instruction and special projects. 5 4 3 2 1

*****

A. List the numbers of items not in compliance. Suggest reasons why they are not.
B. Describe actions that should be taken to reach compliance.

Marc Brackett and Janet Kremenitzer (National Professional Resources Inc. *www.NPRinc.com*) write that:

> *The RULER Approach…supports the power of emotional literacy training. Students trained in emotional literacy showed higher academic grades, higher grades in social development and work habits, were more likely to complete their homework, work cooperatively with others, demonstrate self-control,*

*and pay attention to the rules of the classroom and
the school. (p. xi)*

One of the questions asked by educators is whether or not to
adopt *RULER* if the school or district has an SEL or character development program? *The answer:*

> *RULER integrates seamlessly with many other
> school-based initiatives and its goals and methods
> overlap with those of other SEL and character educa-
> tion programs. In general, RULER becomes the back-
> drop with a common language and a positive and
> safe climate in which to teach other academic and
> SEL topics."* A twelve-page brochure about Ruler
> can be found at http://www.rulerapproach.org.

Your message board

Questions/Thoughts/Ideas/

Character and School Climate

Climate is to a school what character is to an individual!

From what we are hearing and reading from teachers, administrators, students, and parents, we will have to pay close attention to characters' education initiatives and how they affect relationships, learning, teaching, student behaviors, the school's culture and classroom climate.

Research tells the story. "During the COVID-19 period, *seven* out of ten teens reported struggling with *mental health* issues."

> *Our nation's young people are experiencing record levels of anxiety and depression. Mental health researchers have identified social media as the chief cause of the crisis we're in.* (Character.org)

And what about test scores?

> *Students in most states and across almost all demographic groups had experienced troubling setbacks, especially in math, because of the pandemic. The average 13-year-old's understanding of math plummeting back to levels last seen in the 1990s; struggling readers scored lower than they did in 1971, when the test was first administered.*

According to the *National School Climate Center*, school climate improvement work can be grouped into" five *buckets*:

1. Safety
2. Teaching/Learning
3. Institutional environment
4. Interpersonal relations
5. Social media

NSCC notes *that a sustainable, positive school climate fosters youth development and learning necessary for a productive, contributing and satisfying life in a democratic society.*

To know more

> *A White Paper: The School Climate Challenge* By National School Climate Center (NSCC)—Center for Social and Emotional Education (CSEE)—National Center for Learning and Citizenship (NCLC) (*http://nscc.csee.net/ or http://www.ecs.org/school-climate*)

> *School and Classroom Climate Measures* (edited) by Jonathan Schweig, Laura S. Hamilton, Garrett Baker

> *Research confirms the widespread belief that student learning is influenced by features of the school and classroom environments in which instruction takes place. These qualities of the learning environment, often referred to as school and classroom climate, are associated with higher student achievement, improved attendance and graduation rates, and lower rates of suspension. (https://www.rand.org/pubs/research_reports/RR4259.html)*

How to Improve School Climate (edited) *These action items should not be seen as a comprehensive step-by-step approach. (However) they can help teachers, administrators, and other school and district staff plan their efforts to create a positive school climate for all students. Convene a School Climate Team. Gain Stakeholder Buy-in. Use a Data-Informed Approach. Understand the Current Context. Develop a Plan and Select Interventions. Implement and Evaluate. (https://youth.gov/youth-topics/school-climate/ how-to-improve-school-climate)*

School climate attitude scale

Direction to Respondents: After each statement, circle the number indicating the extent to which you (1) Agree; (2) Neutral; (3) Disagree

A) Students are really engaged in this school's character education efforts. 1 2 3
B) This school is a safe place to be. 1 2 3
C) Standards for students' behavior are clear. 1 2 3
D) Core values are modeled and promoted by the adults in this school. 1 2 3
E) Cooperative teaching and learning strategies are used in most classes. 1 2 3
F) Most classes are orderly and free from unnecessary disruptions. 1 2 3
G) Students, faculty, and staff are really engaged in school's character education efforts. 1 2 3
H) This school's character education efforts involve parents and the community. 1 2 3
I) There are high expectations for positive student behaviors. 1 2 3
J) Mutual respect and concern for others is evident in this school. 1 2 3

Two quotes to note

Measuring school climate can help us understand what was and what is, so that we can move forward to what could be.

—H. J. Freiberg, "Measuring School Climate: Let Me Count the Ways," *Educational Leadership*

Strong, positive cultures are places with a shared sense of what is important, a shared ethos of caring and concern, and a shared commitment to helping students learn.

—K. Peterson and T. Deal

Your message board

Questions/Thoughts/Ideas

Character and Emotions

A few months ago, we received this email from a middle grade school teacher:

> *At our school, we do not have resources for our students. The waiting list time for students to have additional support is two months. We have had numerous fights on campus. Our students are angry for a variety of reasons.*
>
> *Two girls had fought others yesterday and again today.*
>
> *This time my colleague tried to intervene and was taken down to the ground by the girls. I went to try to stop it. The students in the hallway were cheering. The reason I am telling you about this situation is that a few of us met and decided that we had to do something to help our students learn to control their emotions instead of "acting out."*
>
> *As you know, we have been using the Center's resources on a regular basis. Two of us attended last month's Saturday Morning Seminar on SEL. It would have been helpful to have more information/discussion on how to help students' handle their emotions.*

> *Can you help us get resources on the topic of students' emotions?*

Our goal was to provide her and her colleagues with hands-on information about emotions—what are the emotions that should be taught and who and how should it be done.

In response to her question, we decided that, among other information, we would say a few words about these four basic emotions: *happiness, fear, sadness, and anger.* We believe that the emotions listed and the resources suggested offers an excellent framework for teachers and others for developing program goals, objectives, units, and lesson plans.

To be sure, we found a *must read* book for you, parents, and others. It is written by Lise Damour, a clinical psychologist specializing in the development of teenage girls and boys.

The title of her book is *The Emotional Lives of Teenagers: Raising Connected Capable and Compassionate Adolescents* (Ballantine Books, 2023).

There are five comprehensive chapters:

One: Adolescent Emotion 101: Getting Past Three Big Myths
Two: Gender and Emotion
Three: How Adolescence Puts a New Emotional Spin on Everyday Life
Four: Managing Emotions: Helping Teens Express Their Feelings
Five: Helping Teens Regain Emotional Control

An article in *ThinkPsych* notes that: *"Emotional intelligence…is a combination of self-awareness and empathy." The article sites these five reasons why emotional learning in children is important:*

1. *Solves underlying problems*
2. *Feeling in control*
3. *Negative emotions lead to negative thoughts*
4. *Form better relationships*

5. *Normalizing feelings reduces anxiety and other health problems (https://thinkpsych.com/blog/teach-children-to-identify-emotions/)*

Another how?

Do you teach your students about emotions? We read psychologist Robert Plutchik's *Wheel of Emotions,* which illustrates the various relationships among these *eight primary emotions*: Anger, Fear, Sadness, Disgust, Surprise, Anticipation, Trust, and Joy (see *https://www.6seconds.org/2022/03/13/plutchik-wheel-emotions/*).

We found a website that you, as a *teacher-leader,* should let the parents in your school know about: *Teaching Children about Emotions Daily/Weekly/Home Ideas.*

We counted over thirty "Daily Ideas," over fifteen "Weekly Ideas," and ten "Home Ideas." *https://www.ecmhc.org/ideas/emotions.html.*

The masks of character

The pandemic is over (almost). Protection masks are off for the most part. We need to change the *mask of protection* to the *masks of character.*

The mask of commitment

The "mask" of *commitment* for students in your classrooms and schools include doing one's duty, being responsible, and being true to one's obligations. Teachers, parents, and other school personnel need to wear these "masks" as well.

The mask of responsibility

Our *responsibility* as teachers and parents is to help young people learn to make good, positive, ethical choices by learning to take *responsibility* for their actions, accepting the rewards, and paying the consequences.

Our *responsibility* as adults is to set examples by being accountable for what we do, what we say, how we act, and how trusting and dependable we are.

A question we should ask those we teach and ourselves is "*What are you responsible for?*"

The mask of kindness

An article in *Scientific American* (February 26, 2009) titled "Forget Survival of the Fittest: It Is Kindness That Counts" features an interview with Dacher Keltner, author of *Born to Be Good: The Science of a Meaningful Life*. Keltner noted that humans have remarkable tendencies "*toward kindness, play, generosity, reverence, and self-sacrifice.*"

In her book, *Kind Is the New Classy*, Candace Cameron Bure writes: "*In this book, we will talk about character traits (love, joy, peace, patience, kindness, goodness, faithfulness, gentleness, and self-control).*"

Her six characteristics for choosing friends are "*friends who are kind, strong, loyal, gentle, encouraging, and principled.*"

The mask of gratitude

Studies have shown that people who experience gratitude have more positive emotions (joy, love, happiness) and exhibit fewer negative emotions (bitterness, envy, resentment). The "*gratitude experience*" contributes to feelings of connectedness, relationships, better physical health, and it also helps people recover more quickly from trauma, adversity, and suffering.

The mask of perseverance

Perseverance is sticking with a course of action despite obstacles. *Perseverance* is a skill that one learns. *Perseverance* builds self-confidence, improves performance, creates trust, helps one work through relationship issues, and opens the door to "resourcefulness."

Perseverance is a key to solving problem and coping with the emotional challenges of school and life.

Angela Duckworth calls the combination of *perseverance and passion—grit.* To encourage "grit" among students, she suggests that teachers "*Model it! Celebrate it! Enable it*"

The mask of empathy

Researchers Dan Goleman and Paul Ekman report that there are three different ways teachers (and others) must address the teaching and learning of empathy:

> *Cognitive empathy: the act of knowing how another person feels. Emotional empathy: the capacity to physically feel the emotions of another. Compassionate empathy: the combination of cognitive and emotional empathy to take action about what one feels and thinks. It is important to help children and youth understand and practice what it means to be empathetic.*

Your message board

Questions/Thoughts/Ideas

Social-Emotional Learning

Here is what we know: Social-emotional skill development is critical to learning and life success in the classroom, community, college, and careers.

Our plan is to share with you a few resources about SEL and its relationship to character education.

The *Collaborative for Academic, Social, and Emotional Learning (CASEL)* plays *the major role* promoting the idea that SEL is central to the educational process in schools across the country. CASEL is the major "go to" organization for SEL information, training, and research. *CASEL's framework connects five broad, interrelated areas of competence: (1) self-awareness, (2) self-management, (3) social awareness, (4) relationship skills, and (5) responsible decision-making (http:// www.helpguide.org/).*

These competencies are *an integral part of education and human development. It is the process through which all young people and adults acquire and apply the knowledge, skills, and attitudes to develop healthy identities, manage emotions and achieve personal and collective goals, feel and show empathy for others, establish and maintain supportive relationships, and make responsible and caring decisions.*

Social Emotional Learning (SEL) programs lead to various short-term and long-term improvements for students that are both immediate and lasting. For example, in our readings, we found the impact of SEL programs to be impressive and includes:

- *students' set high academic goals, receive higher grades and do better academically*
- *students are more self-aware and confident about their learning skills*
- *students' social behaviors and attitude improve*
- *students' negative behaviors and emotional stress are reduced*
- *students' contribute to a safe and orderly classroom/school environment*
- *students' show more positive social behaviors*
- *students' contribute to caring teacher-student and student-student relationships.*
- *students' are able to make responsible decisions, demonstrate self-discipline, motivate themselves, and manage stress.* ("Social and Emotional Learning Research Review," by Vanessa Vega, edutopia, June 2014, *https://www.edutopia. org/sel-research-learning-outcomes*)

To know more

Sara Potler LaHayne writing in *EdSurge poses this question: How can we practice SEL at home?* Here are ten tips that that you should share with parents in your classroom and school.

1. *Take care of yourself, even when it feels like the last thing you can do right now.*
2. *Establish routines and intentionality.*
3. *Presence is not the same as being present.*
4. *Commit acts of service or kindness for others.*
5. *Engage in creativity together.*
6. *Celebrate what you can.*
7. *Practice active listening.*
8. *Help your child express and name emotions.*
9. *Practice social emotional learning daily.*

10. *Transition mindfully. (https://www.edsurge.com/news/2020-04-02-10-ways-parents-can-bring-social-emotional-learning-home)*

Mariah Flynn's article in *Greater Good Magazine* notes that when *students who participated in SEL programs are compared to those who didn't, the results showed significant benefits that persisted from one to nearly four years afterward. These benefits included:*

- *Social and emotional skills, such as identifying emotions, resolving conflicts, and decision-making;*
- *Improved attitudes toward one's self, others, and school;*
- *An increase in positive social behaviors;*
- *Higher grades and achievement test scores;*
- *Fewer conduct problems, including violence, bullying, and classroom disruption;*
- *Lower levels of emotional distress; and*
- *Less substance use. (https://www.linkedin.com/in/mariah-flynn-2819561b/)*

Davidson, Lickona, and Khmelkov (*Education Week*, November 14, 2007) write that

> *[S]tudents need performance character to do their best academic work; (and)…moral character to build the relationships that make for a positive learning environment.*
>
> *Performance character: qualities such as effort, diligence, perseverance, strong work ethic, positive attitude, ingenuity, and self-discipline.*
>
> *Moral character: qualities such as integrity, justice, caring, and respect—these are needed for successful interpersonal relationships and ethical behavior.*

The core virtues of caring, courage, responsibility, respect, empathy, etc., might be the focus in a schools' character education curriculum coupled with attention to academic achievement—school culture and classroom climate, instruction, partnerships, co-curricula programs, special programs. *Each program,* either individually or in combination, would have three goals:

1. the character development of students;
2. the creation of a positive, safe, and nurturing school culture and classroom climate; and
3. the active involvement of educators, parents and the community.

Your message board

Questions/Thoughts/Ideas

Parents/Caregivers

Research shows that when parents/caregivers are active and involved, their children are more likely to:

- have *higher test scores and grade*s,
- develop *greater self-confidence,*
- be *more motivated,*
- have *better social skills*, and
- exhibit *more positive classroom behaviors.*

Reread these "powerful" results. They suggest three key tasks for you to do for your students' parents and caregivers.

Invite, inform, involve!

The importance of relationships, communication, availability, and trust cannot be overstated. As a *character education leader*, you must be active in helping parents/caregivers become involved in and supportive of your school's academic and character efforts.

The question, how? Here are a few suggestions!

One, early in the school year implement: *invite/inform/involve.*

Two, create a communication plan that includes asking parents to tell you the best way(s) to contact them and let them know the best ways they can contact you.

Three, develop a "calendar of classroom events" for each month that Informs parents/caregivers about class activities in which their children will take part. Invite them to attend.

Four, ask parents what they can do at home and/or as a volunteer in your classroom or school to help support character education efforts (involvement).

Five, start an information program (maybe a monthly newsletter) that has character-related themes and questions.

Six, share information about upcoming parent-teacher conferences including the creation of a meeting schedule and possible topics for discussion.

Seven, ask each parent if they would like to have their child participate in a parent-teacher conference.

Eight, invite parents to submit questions they would like discussed at the conference.

THE 3 Is: with this instrument, we (you, parents, administrators, teachers, others) are seeking the opinions of respondents regarding the practices implied by the three words: *invite, inform, involve.*

Directions: Please circle the letter that tells the extent to which you agree with the statement.

A=Agree; B=Neutral; C=Disagree

This school's character education efforts has

1. increased parent/caregiver attendance at parent-teacher meetings. A B C
2. increased parent/caregiver attendance at school events. A B C
3. helped parents/caregivers become more involved in the their child's school work and activities. A B C
4. improve parents/caregivers awareness of their child's behavior at school. A B C
5. increased parents/caregivers support for school's character education programs. A B C

6. encouraged parents/caregivers to help their child practice the core character values/traits at home. A B C
7. strengthened the relationships between teachers and parents/caregiver. A B C

We would appreciate your comments about parental involvement and support of our school's character education efforts. (Please use the back of this form)

To know more

10 Strategies for Schools to Improve Parent Engagement, by Jennifer Larson, *Getting Smart,* October 5, 2019. *https://www.gettingsmart.com/2019/10/05/10-strategies-for-schools-to-improve-parent-engagement/.*
Parent Engagement in Schools, American Psychological Association https://www.apa.org/pi/lgbt/programs/safe-supportive/parental-engagement.
12 Actionable Parent Engagement Strategies for Your K–12 District, by Clay Burnett on March 10, 2020 *https://www.finalforms.com/blog/12-actionable-parent-engagement-strategies-for-your-k-12-district.*

What's love got to do with it?

A History Lesson

Americans probably began exchanging hand-made valentines in the early 1700s. In the 1840s, Esther A. Howland began selling the first mass-produced valentines in America. Howland, known as the "Mother of the Valentine," made elaborate creations with real lace, ribbons and colorful pictures known as "scrap." Today, according to the Greeting Card Association, an estimated 1 billion Valentine's Day cards are sent each year, making Valentine's Day the second largest card-sending holiday of the year. (An estimated 2.6 billion cards are sent for

Christmas.) Women purchase approximately 85 percent of all valentines. https://www.history.com/topics

A Science Lesson

There is an extreme powerful force that, so far, science has not found a formal explanation… This universal force is LOVE…
Love is Light to those who give it and receive it.
Love is Gravity, because it makes some people feel attracted to others.
Love is Power, because it multiplies the best we have, and allows humanity not to be extinguished in their blind selfishness.
Love unfolds and reveals.
For love we live and die.
Love is the most powerful force there is, because it has no limit.
Love is God and God is Love. (From a letter by Albert Einstein to his daughter)

A Question: what is this thing called love?

Psychologist, Barbara Fredrickson, author of the book *Positivity*, writes about "the science of happiness" and focuses on ten positive emotions—love, joy, gratitude, serenity, interest, hope, pride, amusement, inspiration, and awe.

"Love," she writes, *"comes into play in a close and safe relationship. Love is the most common feeling of positivity and comes in surges. Love bonds us to those with whom we have the deepest connections. Love fosters warmth and trust with the people who mean the most to us. Love makes us want to do and be better people."*

We said at the beginning of this chapter that the importance of relationships, communication, availability, and trust cannot be overstated. And with *love* as well! Being "in love" with someone means that you respect him/her; that you are honest, caring, and forgiving. People of character know how to feed all of the attributes of a positive, loving relationship. If this sounds too mushy, we suggest you read Steve Farber's book, *Love Is Just Damn Good Business.*

"Love is not just a greeting-card word and not something to be relegated to your private life. In fact, love is damn good business."

Your message board

Questions/Thoughts/Ideas

The Arts

Musical training is a more potent instrument than any other, because rhythm and harmony find their way into the inward places of the soul, on which they mightily fasten, imparting grace, and making the soul of him who is rightly educated graceful.

—Socrates

Teaching children about art is as important as teaching them math or reading. People see it as a frill, but it's not a frill. It's actually the center of the core. If you cut these out of schools, you are really cutting the heart out of our children and their future.

—Dennis W. Creedon, Assistant Superintendent
in the Philadelphia School District

Creativity and the arts are not just nice to have; they are a necessity. Art creates culture. Culture creates community. And community creates humanity.

—Susan Magsamen, is coauthor (with Ivy Ross) of
Your Brain on Art: How the Arts Transform Us

When we say "the *arts*," we are addressing what one finds in most P–12 schools—*the visual and performing arts,* such as music, dance, theatre, sports, and other school-sponsored student activities.

To know more

In her book, *The Artistic Edge: 7 Skills Children Need to Succeed in an Increasingly Right Brain World,* Lisa Phillips (CEO of Canada's Academy of Stage and Studio Art) notes that there are *seven skills* children and youth learn from the arts.

1. Creative thinking
2. Confidence
3. Problem-solving
4. Relationship building
5. Communication
6. Adaptability
7. Dreaming big (*https://www.tes.com/magazine/sponsored/ artsmark/how-focus-arts-can-boost-resilience-and-character*)

Here is the *San Diego Unified School District Visual and Performing Arts (VAPA)* mission statement:

- *Expands students' capacity to think critically about creative work and artistic processes for self-expression and discovery.*
- *Develops shared understanding among educators, families, and interested parties of how acquired artistic knowledge, skills, and processes impact career paths in and beyond creative industries.*
- *Ensures access to culturally responsive, relevant, and authentic coursework, pathways, instruction, and materials, in all five arts disciplines: dance, media arts, music, theatre, and visual arts.*
- *Builds community in and around schools by engaging all inter-ested parties, allying with the region's economic development, workforce readiness, and higher education, and fostering col-*

> *laborative relationships with the arts community to empower students' civic engagement.*
> * *Take a DIP—Dream, Imagine, Plan.*

Dreams, imagination, and planning are about character. To *do* something with one's dreams, with one's imagination, requires having such character strengths as curiosity, open-mindedness, creativity, persistence, and grit. All necessary skills for "planning."

Ask your students two questions: What do they *dream* about? What do they *imagine*?

In our readings, we discovered that there is a relationship between *dreams and imagination.*

> *Imagination can take you everywhere from anywhere. Everything you see around was once an imagination of someone. Without imagination this world would come to still and there won't be any new inventions. Dreamers change the reality and bring the new way of doing monotonous work. They make people's lives easy with their craft. These imagination quotes will give new dimensions to your creativity. Be curious, be hungry. https://www.overall-motivation.com/*

Zachery Roman writes in his article, "How I'm Encouraging My Kids to Dream Big and Aim High."

> *Take time to ask your child about his or her dreams and see if there are ways you can help your child achieve them. Let your child know that no dream is too big or small to accomplish, but it will take hard work, dedication, and a determination to "leave no stone unturned."*

Interestingly, the American Society of Civil Engineers and the United Engineering Foundation offer a program called *Every Child*

Should Dream Big. These two groups have a *campaign* to place *Dream Big* [imagination] educational toolkits in every US public school, plus many private schools, and schools around the world in countries including Canada, Jamaica, Saudi Arabia, and Madagascar! (*www. discovere.org/dreambig*)

We leave it to you to decide *why* and *how* you might encourage your students, to *dream big*, be *imaginative*, and *plan* carefully.

Your message board

Questions/Thoughts/Ideas

Service Learning

Think of service learning as an educational opportunity by which you and your students learn ways to tackle real-life problems in the school and community.

Think of a service learning program in your school and school district that includes both project-based learning and *problem-based learning*.

Think of service learning that is interdisciplinary, that intellectually challenges your students, giving them a voice and a choice in their learning experiences.

Think of service learning offering programs that develop a range of skills, such as, investigating, discussing, planning, and debating solutions, actions, and reporting results.

Think about service learning where your students are presented with problems and questions that have multiple potential solutions and possibilities for exploration and that supports and enhances:

- using a range of teaching methods and strategies;
- research-based learning;
- learning that develops your students' skills to think critically and creatively when solving problems and making decisions;
- learning that enhances students' communication and collaboration skills;

- opportunities to be a leader and organizer;
- improve your students' academic skills;
- developing students' character strengths;
- developing relationships and contacts with others in the community;
- providing insights about community problems and how to solve them; and
- *enhancing students' sense of being able to accomplish things and claim ownership of their work.*

To know more

> *Six Steps for Successful Service Learning.*
> *Meaningful service: Make sure your project addresses a community need.*
> *Curriculum connections: Apply academic content to practical tasks so students learn by doing.*
> *Student leadership: Help students take ownership of the project.*
> *Reflection: Make meaning of the experience.*
> *Community involvement: Engage community members throughout.*
> *Demonstrate and celebrate: Share the experience with others. (https://www.plt.org/educator-tips/6-steps-for-successful-service-learning/)*

Service Learning Can Be the Bridge to Social Emotional Learning. Educators Should Embrace It (edited) By Scott Petri, a high school history teacher and the 2021 Outstanding California Social Studies Teacher of the Year, *EdSurge,* September 2022. He writes:

> *I have seen firsthand how service-learning engages students as they become leaders in their communities. After taking a closer look at the social emotional learning (SEL) framework, it is clear there is a connection between SEL and service learn-*

ing that educators can use and nurture. Every year, (my) students teach me how service-learning can transform students into agents of change, increasing their leadership skills while improving their communities. Let's empower our teachers to lead the way by embracing an interdisciplinary approach that integrates SEL with service-learning in K-12 education. (https://www.edsurge.com/news/2022-09-06-service-learning-can-be-the-bridge-to-social-emotional-learning-educators-should-embrace-it)

Service learning: questionnaire

What is the impact of the service-learning component on the school's character education initiatives?

School Culture: Has it change for the better?

Classroom Climate: Has it become more civil and caring?

Community: Do recipients of service learning have more favorable views of the school and the students?

Parents: Have parents seen any behavioral changes in their sons/daughters as a result of their participation in service leaning programs?

Curriculum: Has service learning been infused throughout the curriculum including co-curricular offerings?

Instruction: Has service learning instruction capitalized on students as a resource with responsibility for their own learning?

Journaling

Here's a thought: Have you ever felt better just talking about a problem with your friends or parents? Well, consider your *personal journal* as a friend who is always there. You use it or lose it.

We thought that it would be a good idea for students, who are engaged in service learning opportunities, to reflect on and record their experiences.

It appears that *journaling* is part of what some call the "self-care movement."

"Journaling is an outlet for processing emotions and increases self-awareness."

"Writing in no stranger to therapy. Writing's power to heal lies not in pen and paper, but in the mind of the writer."

"A journal is not a record of the minute details of your daily life. Instead, it's a private space for exploring what you think and feel about the people, events, or issues that are important to you."

We were not surprised when we read that the practice of *journaling* may increase "mindfulness, memory, and communication skills" as well as leading to better sleeping habits, greater self-confidence, and a better understanding of one's emotions.

Teachers can use *journaling* as a kind of window into how students are thinking about what they are learning from their assignments, projects, and for assessment purposes.

Journaling service learning experiences might guide students in having more positive and rewarding days.

Journaling service learning experiences invites students to record their thoughts and progress on specific problems or projects.

Journaling service learning experiences might help students develop an "attitude of gratitude."

Your message board

Questions/Thoughts/Ideas

Relationships

Research tells us that few factors in P–12 education have a greater impact on students' educational experiences than a *caring relationship* with teachers and classmates.

James Comer, professor of child psychiatry at Yale University, notes that, "No significant learning can occur without a *significant relationship.*"

We know that *positive relationships* can help reduce the negative effects of stress and boost one's self-esteem.

We know that it starts with the teacher taking time to *build trust* with each student.

We know that trust is a *joint responsibility* between a teacher and his/her students.

We know that paying more attention to developing strong *positive relationships* helps

- reduce student behavior issues,
- improves classroom climate,
- enhances student attitudes and attention, and
- contributes to student achievement.

To know more

Kelly-Ann Allen PhD wrote in the January 2022 issue of *Psychology Today* that "*good relationships with teachers help students feel a greater sense of belonging and connection to the school community.*" She notes that when students feel that they are part of a community at school, they are more likely to engage in positive ways at school.

Dr. Allen poses *three questions:*

Why are relationships in schools important for school belonging?
What are the benefits of positive social interactions for school belonging?
How can school promote a sense of belonging?

Her conclusion: Healthy relationships between students and their peers, teachers, and school staff are key to student belonging. When students feel that they are part of a community at school, they are more likely to participate in school activities, identify with school values, and invest in their work. (https://www.psychologytoday.com/us/blog/ sense-belonging/202201/the-power-relationships-in-schools)

In *Education Week* (www.edweek.org), Sarah D. Sparks wrote an article titled "Why Teacher-Student Relationship Matter." She framed her report around five questions.

1. *Why are student-teacher relationships important?*
2. *How does a teacher's approach affect that relationship?*
3. *How can teachers improve their relationships with students?*
4. *How can teachers maintain healthy boundaries with students?*
5. *How can relationships with students support teacher quality?*

She suggests using this *Student Weekly Check-Up* form on *Relationship (https://www.panoramaed.com/blog/21-questions-check-in-student-sel-wellbeing).*

Also see: Panorama Education, *80 Questions Across Well-Being, SEL Skills, Relationships, and Classroom Feedback.*

We found a recent study that reports that over 1,500 meta-analysis of 90,000 studies involving 300 million students as to what works best in education—*student-teacher relationships* is one of the biggest predictors of success, and *strong classroom cohesion* was found to be just slightly lower.

Questions to ask yourself

How do my interactions (teaching/monitoring/reporting) affect my relationship with students in my class?

Do I respect, care about, and show concern for the character development of my students?

Do I expect that my students will show respect for themselves, their classmates, for me, and for other adults in our school?

Do I find it necessary to improve my relationships with my students? And, if so, what am I going to do about it?

Do I feel that I know how to develop and maintain good relationships with my colleagues, with my students' parents, and others in my school? If not, what do I need to do?

Your message board

Questions/Thoughts/Ideas

Self-Discipline/Self-Management

Character is about consequences—some positive, some negative. *Character is about* people of good character making mistakes.

Character is about people who are self-disciplined and manage emotions and behaviors to hold themselves accountable, take responsibility, and demonstrate perseverance.

Character is about paying the consequences for "negative" behaviors, learn from mistakes, and having the courage to be honest, trustworthy, and compassionate.

Character is about "emotional" *self-discipline and management.*

Recent polls of public attitudes toward schools show that Americans want schools to prepare the young to be *self-disciplined* and reliable, academically competent, and career ready. *Teaching self-management skills to students, at all grade levels, has been proven to improve academic performance, productivity, time-on-task, and decrease problem behavior.*

You should know that there are three types of discipline:

Preventive Discipline—preempt misbehavior;

Supportive Discipline—teachers assist students with self-control; and

Corrective Discipline—when students are not following classroom or school rules teachers do something about it.

You should know that research suggests that students who learn self-discipline strategies are more responsible, respectful, and self-reliant.

You should know that being taught self-discipline skills and develops students' analytical skills, helps them make better decisions, and contributes to a better understanding and appreciation for will-power, hard work, and persistence.

You should know the answer to the question, *how?*

Based on our experiences and our research, we found that when teaching students how to discipline themselves, these teaching strategies work best:

- Start early.
- Have rules.
- Have routines.
- Have rewards and consequences.
- Employ time management activities.
- Help students see mistakes as opportunities.
- Encourage the proper use of discipline techniques.
- Suggest ways to take time-outs and exercise breaks.

To know more

"8 Ways to Teach Kids Self-Discipline Skills" by Amy Morin, LCSW/Verywell Mind/TRUSTe/2023/edited):

1. *Self-discipline helps kids delay gratification.*
2. *When helping kids learn how to make healthy choices, an authoritative approach is best because it helps kids understand the reasons for the rules.*
3. *Sometimes, natural consequences can teach some of life's greatest lessons. At other times, kids need logical consequences.*
4. *Any time your child is learning a new skill or gaining more independence, help them do so one small step at a time.*
5. *Giving kids praise for making good choices increases the likelihood that they'll repeat that behavior.*

6. *Teach problem-solving skills and work together to correct specific issues related to self-discipline.*
7. *Make it a priority to model self-discipline.*
8. *Reward systems should be short-term. (https://www.verywellfamily.com/teach-kids-self-discipline-skills-1095034)*

Teaching Self-Management Skills: 5 Strategies to Create an Effective Plan (edited), *Positive Action Staff/* August 2020.

What is a self-management plan? Teaching self-management skills for students has been proven to improve academic performance, productivity, time-on-task, and decrease problem behavior.

Goal setting: students and teachers should cooperate in setting small, reachable goals that the student can work toward.

Behavior monitoring: self-monitoring or behavior monitoring occurs when students observe and record their behaviors, redirecting themselves when necessary.

Self-reinforcement: self-reinforcement is the act of rewarding oneself after completing the desired behavior or meeting a goal.

Self-evaluation: the process also teaches students the power of resilience and perseverance. They learn that failure can happen, but if they keep trying, they can succeed.

Build an effective teaching plan with these five strategies:

1. *Time Management Logs.*
2. *Checklists and Rubrics.*
3. *Rating scales.*
4. *Contracts or agreement*
5. *Behavior report cards.*

Apology, forgiveness, gratitude, love

One of the characters in the book *The Hummingbird* by Stephen P Kiernan (Harper Collins Publishers, 2015) asks another character, *"What would be your answer to each of these four questions?"*

Is there anyone you need to say "I'm sorry" to? Is there anyone you need to say "I forgive you" to? Is there anyone you need to say "Thank you" to? Is there anyone you need to say "I love you" to?

We were struck by the power of the four questions and what they say about *reflection*, something we do often in our classrooms. Let's start with *apology*: *"How to apologize can be the key to getting true forgiveness and moving a relationship forward in a positive way,"* writes Marlee McKee. McKee offers seven tips for apologizing sincerely and successfully:

1. *Ask for permission to apologize.*
2. *Let them know that you realize you hurt them.*
3. *Tell them how you plan to right the situation.*
4. *Let them know that in your apology is a promise that you won't do what you did again.*
5. *After you've talked through things, formally ask them for forgiveness.*
6. *Consider following up with a handwritten note.*
7. *Now it's time for both people to go forth and live out their promises.* (https://www.mannersmentor.com/gracious-living/how-to-apologize-the-7-steps-of-a-sincere-apology)

Forgiveness: Teaching children "forgiveness" as you may have guessed, is a parent and teacher responsibility. Enright and Fitzgibbons write that *"forgiveness is a virtue hard to exercise and challenging to implement in the face of injustice, but one that offers a concrete hope for peace."* They recommend *"family forgiveness gatherings"* at least once a week, such as during mealtimes, to talk about *"what forgiveness means, how it feels, and what is easy and hard about."*

Jamie Perillo, LPC, a child and family psychotherapist and parent educator, notes that we look beyond the action and explore the person—helping her/him to answer the question: *"What triggered the behavior?"*

"We need to teach our kids to be able to see things from the other side. Forgiving is much easier when we know the whole story and not just half of it. Ask your kids how they would want someone to respond when

they did something wrong. They would want to be forgiven. Then tell them to do likewise." (https://psychcentral.com/blog/how-to-teach-a-child-forgiveness/)

Gratitude (Thanks): Robert A. Emmons, PhD, the world's leading scientific expert on gratitude, said: *"You literally cannot overplay the hand of gratitude; the grateful mind reaps massive benefits in every domain of life that has been examined so far. There are countless ways in which gratitude could pay off in the workplace"* (and in homes and schools). The "gratitude experience" contributes to feelings of connectedness, relationships, and better physical health.

Love: Barbara Fredrickson, psychologist and author of the book *The Science of Happiness,* discusses ten positive emotions *including love.* "Love," she writes, *"comes into play in a close and safe relationship. Love is the most common feeling of positivity and comes in surges. Love fosters warmth and trust with the people who mean the most to us. Love makes us want to do and be better people."*

This might be a good time for you to reflect on each of the four questions and plan your next steps. Take ten minutes and ask yourself, "Is there anyone I need to say *I'm sorry, I forgive you, I thank you, I love you* to?"

Your message board

Questions/Thoughts/Ideas

Restorative Justice

There are several reasons for implementing "restorative justice strategies" in schools. One is promoting *better student behavior*. A second is to *involve students* in assessing and examining negative behaviors (what happened and why). A third is to *give students a voice* in consequences (punishments) for negative behavior(s). A fourth reason is to *create a positive school/classroom environment*.

The International Institute for Restorative Practices list these *five Rs* for restorative justice programs and practices: *Relationship, Respect, Responsibility, Repair, Reintegration*.

They note that:

> *"Restorative practices" focuses on repairing harm through inclusive processes that bring together students and educators. The intention of restorative justice is to shift the focus of student discipline from punishment to reflecting learning, emphasizing accountability, making amends, and facilitating dialogue between affected parties. Restorative school discipline practices focus on fostering a sense of community within classrooms to prevent conflict, and on reacting to misconduct by encouraging students to accept responsibility and rebuild relationships. The three core elements of restor-*

> *ative justice are: Encounter, Repair, and Transform.*
> *(https://www.iirp.edu/)*

In our readings and discussions with colleagues, we found that *Restorative Justice* practices and programs use individual and group sessions (circles) to help students resolve conflicts on their own with a mediator and or in small groups rather than resorting to suspensions or expulsions.

As expected, we found an emphasis on school districts' teachers and counselors being trained to help students on how best to help their *peers resolve conflicts* through communication, problem solving, accountability, and concrete actions.

Our summary: RJ is about the teaching and learning of *character strengths* such as respect, responsibly, kindness, empathy, and self-discipline.

RJ is also about *relationships*—building and repairing them.

We found that several RJ programs stressed that mediators "use non-blaming restorative questions when discussing any behavior or issue with students."

Here are a few "*restorative* questions" you could ask a student when he/she is "in trouble":

Why are you here?
Tell me what happened?
When did it happen?
How did it happen?
Why did it happen?
What was your part in what happened?
Who were the others affected by what you did?
What were you thinking when what you did happened? What do you think about it now?
What do you think is the best way to solve this problem/this conflict?
What should you do to repair the harm you caused?
What do you need to do to make things right?

What's your plan?
Who do you suggest will help you carry out your plan?

To know more

8 Tips for Schools Interested in Restorative Justice, Fania E. Davis, Co-Founder and Executive Director, Restorative Justice for Oakland Youth, September 26, 2014 (edited):

> *Here are eight tips if your school seeks to launch a Restorative Practice Program.*
>
> 1.   *Assess Need*
> 2.   *Engage the School Community*
> 3.   *Hire a Restorative Justice Coordinator*
> 4.   *Begin Training*
> 5.   *School-Wide Implementation*
> 6.   *Institute Restorative Discipline*
> 7.   *Involve Students in Peer Restorative Practices*
> 8.   *Be Sure to Evaluate (https://www.edutopia. org/blog/restorative-justice-tips-for-schools- fania-davis)*

Using Restorative Justice to Transform School Culture by Matt Homrich-Knieling, *edutopia,* July 20, 2022 (edited):
Here are some of my key takeaways from my experience as a middle school restorative justice coordinator. *Restorative Justice Is Not a Behavior Management Technique:* If we see restorative practices as strategies to help us build real relationships and address harm, we will have the tools necessary to address conflicts that will inevitably occur.

Restorative circles: Restorative circles can be used as proactive relationship-building strategies *Restorative Justice Requires Challenging Power Dynamics Between Students and Teachers.*

How can we create space for students to feel safe to address conflicts with adults in school?

Restorative justice requires a root-cause analysis

What are the conditions (practices, rules, beliefs, etc.) that might lead to harm or conflict in your classroom and your school? What power do you have to transform those conditions? (*https://www.edutopia.org/article/using-restorative-justice-transform-school-culture*)

Restorative justice practices in afterschool programs

A Briefing Paper (twenty-six pages) by Sam Piha and Samantha Fasen, The How Kids Learn Foundation (HKLF), is a 501(c)(3) organization. It is dedicated to improving the effectiveness of settings that support the education and healthy development of youth. This includes schools and out-of-school time programs.

> *HOW TO USE THIS BRIEFING PAPER: This paper is designed to raise understanding and awareness of restorative justice practices and identify ways afterschool leaders can integrate them. We recommend that program leaders share this paper with organizational leaders and program staff and consider the best ways to respond to personal harm and conflicts among youth participants. (https://www. eventbrite.com/e/restorative-justice-practices-in-afterschool-programs-tickets-692070329987)*

> *Restorative circles play an important role in addressing challenges that students face. Begin by creating a safe space for students to learn empathy, patience, and compassion for others. Use your students' input to decide which topics of discussion they want to address, such as mutual respect and problems surrounding racism. Help students build community through restorative circles and make them more proactive when it comes to developing meaningful connections and promote healing.*

(https://www.prodigygame.com/main-en/blog/ restorative-practices-in-schools/)

Restorative justice can serve as an indispensable tool for achieving these goals. Restorative justice focuses on the interrelatedness of the human experience and offers an alternative framework for resolving conflict and the resulting harm. It seeks to address the question of how to "make things right." Restorative justice draws upon principles of community-building, reconciliation, and peacemaking. (Dr. Artika Tyner, *The Inclusive Leader*)

Your message board

Questions/Thoughts/Ideas

Social Skills

Social skills should be an important part of your school's character education program. You need to take a leadership role to be sure that social skills, like other character traits, are *taught, modeled, strengthened, and practiced.*

Teaching your students social skills is about helping them learn these "how-tos":

- be a friend,
- use effective and respectful communication,
- feel and show empathy for others,
- appreciate others,
- be polite, respectful, courteous,
- resolve conflicts peacefully,
- follow directions,
- respect others' personal space,
- use good manners,
- promote positive interactions with others,
- find polite ways to assert yourself when it is appropriate,
- communicating clearly, and showing respect for others.
- work with others (teamwork),
- create positive relationships and repair broken ones,
- listen carefully and accurately,
- predict others' feelings and reactions, and

- respect diverse viewpoints and, if necessary "respectfully" disagree.

The Positive Action Staff created a list of thirteen *ways you can use to teach social skills to your students and help them learn new social techniques more quickly and effectively.*

1. *Work with peer mentors*
2. *Adopt a research-based program*
3. *Model social skills with videos*
4. *Use film and video clips*
5. *Have Students create videos*
6. *Imitate and model other students*
7. *Construct social narratives*
8. *Create lunch groups*
9. *Form structured social situations*
10. *Encourage communication with joint action routines*
11. *Create a classroom management plan*
12. *Encourage teamwork*
13. *Social role-play activities*

The staff notes that "a lack of social skills can contribute to poor academic performance, causing problem behaviors in class and dropping grades." (*https://www.positiveaction.net/blog/ways-to-teach-social-skills*)

Here are a few questions that you as a *"character education teacher leader"* should be asking.

Is there anything on the lists (above) that my students need to learn and that I and others should be teaching?

What social skills am I currently teaching my students?

What are the social skills being taught in other classrooms in this school?

What are the most effective ways to teach students social skills?

How does social skill development relate to my students' attitudes and habits (heart/mind/hands)?

Am I involving parents and families in helping me teach their children social skills?

What am I and my colleagues doing to find out if our "efforts" to teach our students social skills are "paying off"?

Students' prosocial behaviors perception checklist

Suggestion: administer this checklist to as many stakeholders as reasonable.

Question: since this school has implemented a character education program, how many students now exhibit/demonstrate/practice the following prosocial/proactive behaviors.

Scale: answer the questions below using this scale:

MOST—MANY—SOME— FEW

More respectful?
More responsible?
More caring?
More cooperative?
Show less at-risk behaviors?
More engaged in class work?
More interested in taking leadership responsibilities?
More willing to confront bullying issues?
More positive relationship among students?
Less substance abuse?
Greater enjoyment in school activities?
More student volunteers in school and in the community?
Greater appreciation of each other's differences?

The skills game

A "skills" quote: *"Expressing care for another is not an innate ability present more naturally in some people than others, but rather a skill that can be taught and nurtured through a supportive educational environment"* (Scotty McLennan, Dean for Religious Life, Stanford University (emphasis added).

At a recent meeting with teachers, we started talking about "twenty-first-century skills." Our view is that there is not enough attention given to helping students develop their *social skills*.

Recent surveys showed that employers are looking for these social skill qualities in employees: listening and communication *skills*, adaptability, creative thinking *skills*, problem-solving *skills*, goal setting *skills,* and competence in reading, writing, and computation *skills*. It has been reported that 85 percent of those who lose jobs do so because of inadequate *social skills*.

Social skill development should be an essential part of a school's character education program. *A survey conducted through Pew Research Center's American Trends Panel asked this question: What are the best skills for kids to have these days?* The responses:

    90 percent—Communication
    86 percent—Reading
    79 percent—Math
    77 percent—Teamwork
    75 percent—Writing
    74 percent—Logic
    58 percent—Science
    25 percent—Athletics
    24 percent—Music
    23 percent—Art

Social skills include habits and attributes that some call *habits of the heart.* This includes providing instruction and practice in helping students to be respectful, responsible, honest, trustworthy, caring, courageous, courtesy, compassionate, and fair.

These learned skills are pled with *habits of the mind*—being a critical thinker, appreciating the importance of knowledge and learning, learning how to learn, practicing self-discipline, making ethical decisions, learning to problem solve, controlling anger and emotions, resisting peer pressure, and thinking before acting.

The third skill set is often labeled, *habits of the hands,* which includes knowing and practicing the Golden Rule, being of service to others, and becoming an active, participating citizen.

In our research, we found a program developed by Stephen Elliott (Vanderbilt Peabody education and psychology researcher) and coauthored with Frank Gresham of the newly published *The Social Skills Improvement System Classwide Intervention Program (SSIS-CIP).*

They identified the top ten skills that students need to succeed based on surveys of over eight thousand teachers and over twenty years of research in classrooms across the country. The skills are:

> *Listen to others*
> *Follow the steps*
> *Follow the rules*
> *Ignore distractions*
> *Ask for help*
> *Take turns when you talk*
> *Get along with others*
> *Stay calm with others*
> *Be responsible for your behavior*
> *Do nice things for others*

They report:

> *In our research, we found that elementary kids and teachers value cooperation and self-control. When we teach and increase those behaviors, we reduce problem behaviors and maximize learning time…*
>
> *If we increase social skills, we see commensurate increases in academic learning. That doesn't mean that social skills make you smarter; it means that these skills make you more amenable to learning.*

More information about the SSIS Program can be found at: *http://www.PearsonAssessments*.com.

Another discovery—a website called SKILLSYOUNEED (*https://skillsyouneed.com*), which provides information and resources for each of the following category of skills: personal, interpersonal, leadership, learning, presentation, writing, numeracy, and parenting skills.

And, finally, think about this each month during the school year: *"Children who scored high on social skills were four times as likely to graduate from college than those who scored low." (Teaching Social Skills to Improve Grade and Lives*, David Bornstein, *http://opinionator. blogs.nytimes.com/2015/07/24)*

Your message board

Questions/Thoughts/Ideas

Teaching Patience

When teaching students how to be *patient,* there are four inter-related factors that need your attention. They are: patience, practice, perseverance, promises. *Patience* is a skill that all students have to practiced and reinforced. Learning how to be patient helps students develop a sense of delayed gratification. Learning to be patient helps students deal with "self-control" issues regarding their actions, their time, their mistakes, their responsibilities, and their relationships with schoolmates, friends, and family.

The dictionary defines the word *practice* as "the act of doing something regularly or repeatedly to improve your skills at doing it." Your students probably know what it means because they use it when doing school assignments. What you will be teaching them is how best to *practice* being patience and why.

Some educators define *perseverance* as having "grit"—the patience to plan long-term goals, being a hard worker, able to finish what one begins, always trying to improve, and not being discouraged by setbacks.

Promises means that a person agrees, assures, guarantees, and makes a commitment to what he/she promised to do.

To know more

"10 Teaching Patience Activities for Kids (Edited)," by Michael Vallejo, LCSW/*mentalhealthcenterkids*/April, 2023:

> *Encouraging Middle and High School Students to Build Patience in the Classroom* (edited *3 Ways to Encourage Students to Develop Patience (1) Give them time. I typically dedicate at least the first 1 to 2 minutes as silent work time so that the students have a chance to read the directions and make a first attempt at the assignment. (2) Give them criteria. I outline for students what must be done before they can ask for help. (3) Give them an option. To help these students build their ability to remain patient in the classroom, have options in place for them while they wait.* Tell students what their options are for when they're either waiting for help or if they finish their work early. *(https://www.edu-topia.org/article/encouraging-middle-and-high-school-students-build-patience-classroom/)*

From the Peaceful Parent Institute!

This is an article you may want to share with your students' parents if they want their teenager to be patient, reasonable, and understanding. It is written by Genevieve Simperingham. Here are a few important considerations in her blog.

1. It's not enough to listen, we need to show that we've understood.
2. Our empathy helps them develop patience.
3. Emotional safety promotes mental health.
4. Things can easily things can" go south."
5. A child's emotional intelligence develops slowly over time.
6. Maturity doesn't just come with age.

7. Help your kid develop consideration for you and others.

She notes: *These are such simple but very important human needs, which create a lot of satisfaction when met. Yet a lot of frustration when not met (https://www.peacefulparent.com/if-you-want-your-teenager-to-be-patient-reasonable-and-understanding/).*

Your message board

Questions/Thoughts/Ideas

Finding a Purpose

Let's start with the question, what does purpose mean? Here are some descriptors we found that describe the need for and importance of having a purposeful life.

Purpose:

is a character strength
is associated with motivation;
creates a sense of social responsibility;
helps develop one's since of happiness;
provides one with a sense of direction;
grows from our connection to others;
contributes to academic achievement;
changes as we age;
is a "journey and a practice"; and
a "fundamental component of a fulfilling life."

"Most young people and even most adults don't have a purpose in their life. Most students experiences are oriented around external achievement, checking off boxes, and short-term goal fulfillment," says, Kendall C. Bronk, an associate professor of developmental psychology at Claremont Graduate University in California.

His research suggests that "finding one's purpose requires four key components:

1.   *dedicated commitment,*
2.   *personal meaningfulness,*
3.   *goal directedness, and*
4.   *a vision larger than one's self.*

These are skills that should be taught in our classrooms and nurtured in our schools.

To know more

"Five Ways to Help Students Build a Strong Sense of Purpose (Edited)," by Lauren Faggella, *Summit Learning,* February 2018:

> *Here are five ways that all educators—from professional teachers to parents to local business owners—can play an essential role in helping young people develop a strong Sense of Purpose.*
>
> 1.   *Build Self-Awareness Early*
> 2.   *Serve as Models and Mentors*
> 3.   *Expose Students to Real-World Learning*
> 4.   *Ask Good Questions*
> 5.   *Give Students Voice and Choice (https://blog. summitlearning.org/)*

> *Tips to Guide Teens To Find Purpose in Life Center for Parent and Teen Communication, Character Strengths,* November 2018

> *1. Help Teens Understand How Much They Matter 2. Celebrate Unevenness 3. Have Small, Frequent Conversations with Teens 4. Model a Life of Purpose, Joy, and Fulfillment 5. Provide Opportunities for Exploration 6. Encourage Volunteer*

Work 7. Be Patient! https://parentandteen.com/ tips-guide-teens-purpose/

Seven Tips to Start (and Continue) the Conversation 1. Help Teens Understand How Much They Matter 2. Celebrate Unevenness 3. Have Small, Frequent Conversations with Teens 4. Model a Life of Purpose, Joy, and Fulfillment 5. Provide Opportunities for Exploration 6. Encourage Volunteer Work 7. Be Patient!

This article was written by Shannon Traurig, a former graduate student at CPTC, with contributions from Expert Advisory Board member, Dr. William Damon. *https://parentandteen.com/ tips-guide-teens-purpose/*

On Purpose

The importance of and need for developing a sense *purpose* in children and youth is new to us, as it may be for you. We used *The Journal of Character Education* (V15-N2, 2019) to help us get a sense of what *purpose* is about. Let's start with the question, what does *purpose* mean?

The *Journal* editors write: "*We are aware that motivation is central to the foundation of character, and particularly moral character. Purpose lies at the heart of such motivation [and] is central to the heart by being a core of the motivational impetus to be good.*"

Several articles in the *Journal* addressed the meaning of *purpose*. A few examples:

"*Purpose has been associated with increased hope and life satisfaction, positive affect, academic achievement, and with life transitions from early adolescence through emerging adulthood."*

"Purpose is a character strength, or virtue, that is vital to individual well-being and healthy communities."

"Defining purpose as a beyond the self-life goal suggests that purposeful people are aware of the perspective of others, have some well-developed other-oriented values, such as compassion, justice, equality, and have a sense of social responsibility."

"The potential for purpose emerges with the development of moral emotions and reasoning, future-mindedness, and the capacity to act on higher-order goals."

"A definition of purpose includes three keys dimensions: (1) purpose as a sense of direction, (2) purpose that is personally meaningful, and (3) purpose as a desire to make a difference on the broader world."

Kendall C. Bronk's (Associate Professor of Developmental Psychology at Claremont Graduate University): *"Review of the purpose literature concluded that the majority of definitions consists of three irrefutable components: commitment, goal-directedness, and personal meaningfulness."*

We want to briefly report on three articles. One addresses instruction (practices) and two that describe curriculum (programs).

Quinn, Heckes, and Shea write about classroom practices supporting the development of *purpose* among adolescents. In summary, the most common teacher-practice was *"the identification of a goal or long-term intention in the classroom including encouragement, teacher-set goals, student-set goals, and goals set by both."* In order to help students find personal meaning, teachers most frequently utilized the following strategies: *"making outward connections, attending to students' interests, establishing a strong teacher-student relationship, and making content interesting… (including) using projects and group work, teaching life skills, making outward connections, and civics education."*

Stillman and Martinez's article offers a "practitioner perspective" using a Six Seconds EQ Model (know/choose/give). The inner circle of the framework included these skills: *"know yourself, choose yourself, and give yourself";* and three competencies: enhancing emotional literacy/recognize patterns; consequential thinking/navigate emotions/intrinsic motivation/optimism; increase empathy/pursue noble goals. The EQ Model asked students to think about three questions: *"What am I feeling? What options do I have? What do I truly want?"*

The MPOWER program (Klein, et.al.) is a school program designed to promote *purpose* by *"helping students connect to supportive people, identify their passion and core values, and discover their strengths."* The program's primary thrust is to engage students in *"grappling"* with three essential questions: *"What do they want to achieve? Who do they want to become? How do they lead purposeful lives?"* The 4-Ps of MPOWER are: *"people, passion, propensity, and pro-social benefits.*

In December 2023, Angela Duckworth, the cofounder of Character Lab and professor at the University of Pennsylvania, posted two reports about *purpose* (edited). In the first report, she defined *purpose as a commitment to making a meaningful contribution to the world." She wrote that:*

> *[H]aving a purpose is good for both you and the world; that it drives you to make positive contributions in line with your own interests and strengths… It motivates and guides your short-term goals and daily activities. You enjoy a more meaningful life, (are) more resilient to setbacks, (area) more energetically, and feel good about what you've accomplished.*

Professor Duckworth asks these questions:

> How *true (are) the following for you?*

I look for ways to have positive effects on others' lives.

I often reflect on my life goals and the kind of person I want to be.

When I plan out my day, I consider how my activities connect to what I want to accomplish with my life. I often think about what I can offer the world, taking into account what the world needs as well as my personal strengths and interests.

I often think about what matters most to me and why it matters.

To encourage a sense of *purpose* in young people, she suggests that we:

> *Model it. Engage in activities that connect to your own purpose, such as meaningful work, volunteering, or creating art—and invite young people to participate with you. Celebrate it. Praise and support actions that serve a larger purpose: Point out connections between activities and long-term goals.*
>
> *Enable it. Encourage young people to talk about their values and the kind of person they want to be. What do they want to contribute to the world? No matter their age, children can be helpful to others.*

One week later, in her second posting on the topic, Professor Duckworth invited Scott Barry Kaufman, host of *The Psychology Podcast,* to talk about *purpose.* Here are a few highlights:

> How do you define purpose, and why is it important?
>
> *I define purpose as having an energizing goal that is meaningful to you. The goal itself is energizing, not depleting. You want to do it.*

How can parents and teachers help young people think about purpose?

Parents and teachers can ask questions that help kids figure out what's most important to them. Example: When you wake up in the morning, what are some of the first things you think about that you're excited about doing during your day? Questions help disentangle what goals they feel they should have versus the goals they genuinely want to have.

Does focusing on your own goals make you selfish?

Finding your purpose can help you think beyond the self and connect to the larger world. What do people often get wrong about purpose? I think we should all—from teachers to parents to even friends—try to spot the potential and the seeds of a higher purpose that are often quite evident but ignored. The more we help kids focus and channel their energy, opinions, and thoughts, the better.

Your message board

Questions/Thoughts/Ideas

Setting Goals

Why should you and your students set goals?

Goal-setting contributes to your students' character and achievement. It is a character-builder helping students develop such traits as curiosity, persistence, creativity, self-discipline, responsibility, reflection, adaptability, and decision-making.

Goal-setting needs to be taught, modeled, and practiced in your classroom. It requires self-discipline, time, and patience.

Goal setting helps your students develop a "plan for action" both short long-range plans.

Goal setting helps your students develop their time-management skills and how best to stay on track.

Goal setting helps guide your students in the choices they make, the confidence they build, and the relationships they develop.

Goal setting helps engage both you and your students in planning lessons and developing student activities.

To encourage and engage your students in carefully planning their goals, you should guide them in answering the following questions:

- *Why* is this goal important to you?
- *Who* will you ask to help you with this goal?
- Have you shared this goal with your teacher, classmates, and others to get their advice help and support?

- *What* do you hope to accomplish?
- *What* resources will you need?
- *When* do you want to accomplish this goal?
- *What* do you need to do to track your progress toward reaching this goal?
- *How* will you know when you have reached your goal?

Another "question-asking" strategy was developed in 1981 by George T. Doran who created S.M.A.R.T. goals. In addition to the questions we listed above, you should also teach your students how to be "S.M.A.R.T." when planning a goal.

Specific: What do you want to achieve?
Measurable: How will you measure your progress?
Attainable: What do you need in order to achieve your goal?
Relevant: Why do you want to achieve this goal?
Timely: What's your (realistic) deadline for your goal?

To know more

Goal-Setting for Students, Kids, and Teens: Learning how to set goals in school and seeing goal setting modeled by peers and teachers is a great way to encourage effective goal setting in children (https://positivepsychology.com/goal-setting-students-kids/).

"6 Activities That Inspire a Goal-Setting Mindset in Students" by Paige Tutt, edutopia, March 2022:

> Here are six activities to help scaffold the process of goal setting, providing students with a deeper understanding of how to recognize when they need to set a goal, how to think about their own progress, and how to move forward when they encounter hurdles along the way:
>
> 1. Start early and take your time.
> 2. Keep it simple.

3. Tap into dreams.
4. Make goal-setting visual.
5. Set stretch goals.
6. Imagine the goal and the hurdles. (https://www.edutopia.org/article/6-activities-inspire-goal-setting-mindset-students/)

We recommend that you look at character.org's two award winning programs that will help inform you and others about your character education goals and assessment efforts?

Promising Practices and National Schools of Character—In 2021, for example, 47 schools and 1 school district won awards. There is a rigorous goal-setting and evaluation process. There are standards that must be met, and each award-winning school/districts has put into place a comprehensive approach that inspires their students to understand, care about and consistently practice a set of core values that will enable them to flourish in school, in relationships, in the workplace, and as citizens. (https://www.character.org/schools-of-character/)

Your message board

Questions/Thoughts/Ideas

Getting Motivated

You should know that "students who are motivated are more likely to set goals and work toward achieving those goals. Students are more likely to have *higher achievement and learn more* when they are motivated."

To *motivate* your students, you should:

- Know your students;
- Get them engaged and involved in being role models and mentors;
- Organize your students in small groups and teams to foster motivation and collaboration;
- Encourage setting goal-setting, planning, and checking progress;
- Give them feedback on the work they do, how they do it and encourage self-reflection;
- Give students options and decision-making opportunities;
- Encourage them to become involved in family and community matters;
- Vary your classroom routines, responsibilities and student management assignments; and
- Use technology to increase student interests and interactions.

Many experts suggest that the best ways to *motivate* students is to

- help them see the *purpose* in what they are learning,
- help them *learn subject matter,*
- help them learn about *character-building behaviors,*
- help them earn the importance of *relationships,*
- help them learn to be *responsible* and *respectful,*
- relate learning to the *real-world* outside the classroom,
- help student take advantage of *internships* and other *career-connected* learning,
- *praise* them and reward them for work well-done
- help them develop a sense responsibility and control
- encourage them to work together in and out of the class-room, and
- help them manage their anxieties and "stress points."

To Know More

"11 (More) Tips to Encourage Unmotivated Students (Edited)" by Erin Walton, *Teaching Tips*:

> *No single idea is a game-changer on its own; but when used consistently, these are great for putting a smile on those "down" students, and helping them move forward.*
>
> *Incorporate peer feedback, self-evaluation, or a sharing moment when students can tell the class about something they achieved or are proud of that week.*

1. *Better student self-talk.*
2. *Stay motivated yourself.*
3. *Work to your students' interests.*
4. *Change layout regularly.*
5. *Know what to say.*
6. *Provide a "why."*
7. *Encourage goal-setting.*

8.   *Be clear with instructions.*
9.   *Lean into competition.*
10. *Leave the textbook aside.*
11. *Give "the right" feedback (https://teacherblog. ef.com/encourage-unmotivated-students/).*

"Proof Points: What Almost 150 Studies Say about How to Motivate Students (Edited)," by Jill Barshay, *The Hechinger Report*, September 2021.

> Researchers found 144 studies "on sparking student motivation" involving nearly 80,000 students, from elementary school through university.
>
> Two conclusions:
>
> One, teachers are far more influential than parents in motivating students to learn" (maybe a result of the fact that) "the teacher has more tools to work with for student motivation.
>
> Two, the way that teachers and parents influence motivation is an indirect one, by satisfying three psychological needs, competency, belonging and autonomy. A sense of competence rose to the top for helping kids feel motivated to learn (because) students who have a strong sense of competence are likely to think that they'll get better grades if they study or they'll succeed if they do an exercise.

Recommendation to teachers

> *Listen to the thoughts and feelings of students and respond to them with empathy. Explain rules and requirements so that students can understand why they're being asked to do them. Give students choices and allow them to personalize assignments. For example, teachers might allow students to come up with their own writing topics or devise their own scientific experiment.*

> *Help your students develop positive thinking skills. Teach your students to be grateful because people who are grateful have more positive emotions and fewer negative emotions.*

Praise as a motivator

A favorite middle school teacher of ours expressed her concern that we do not "praise" students enough. We responded to her concern by doing some research. We found out that "praise" is a *powerful motivator,* that praise can improve students' *academic performance,* and that praise contributes to students' *positive behaviors.*

All learning is effortful, so when students display willingness and success, they deserve to be acknowledged. When children feel proficient in something, they develop a greater sense of agency and are therefore more curious about the next aspect of their learning.

We should secure success early and often so that students feel empowered and confident when navigating future learning. Recognition also makes us feel good. It helps to boost our self-esteem and our sense of self-worth. (Hannah Hawthorne, "Understanding the Importance of Motivation in Education," *High Speed Training,* November 2021)

> *Motivation and commitment are both required for success. Commitment is fueled by motivation--the fuel that drives your action. It is the hard work we need to put in... This path is not possible without motivation. Once we move beyond motivation and literally act, it is commitment.*

> —Paulette Rao, ICF Registered Mentor Coach

Your message board

Questions/Thoughts/Ideas

Expectations

We begin by reporting on a survey of executives in twelve of the "nation's leading companies (see the March 2021 issue of *Education Week* by Mark Lieberman) titled "US Companies: Key Job Skills Students Need Post-Pandemic" (www.edweek.orgl; edited).

The executives were asked: "*Tell us what you'll want and expect from today's K–12 students when you eventually hire them…*

We have selected excerpts from each of nine executives that address our *expectation* theme.

> *(1) Schools should provide quality, universal pre-K education that is consistent for all children… Ensure that every child can read before 3rd grade.*
>
> *(2) To prepare students for the effective teamwork they will need in the workforce, schools can focus on teaching coaching, collaboration, motivating different personalities, fostering inclusiveness, and resolving conflict.*
>
> *(3) It would appear that the skills that will have the greatest impact in the modern workplace are… critical thinking, creativity, cognitive flexibility and self-regulation.*
>
> *(4) Students need help developing a growth mindset, becoming more self-directed and disci-*

plined, learning to prioritize, and overall more digital fluency.

(5) With the onset of the COVID-19 pandemic, the skills of empathy, openness to continued growth, and self-motivation as well as the ability to express oneself have become increasingly more important and need to be continually developed.

(6) Students today need to develop and refine skills to communicate clearly, concisely, (through a host of mobile and digital platforms) and with intention in their work, client, and personal relationships, through courses focusing on presentation skills, effective writing, and more.

(7) It's critical that today's students have the support they need... Teachers, coaches, and parents play a critical role by encouraging resilience-building factors: practicing good physical and mental health, staying active and practicing stress-reduction activities, building connections...

(8) We've been inspired by their (teachers) dedication to help students engage and build community, to have conversations about race and social justice, to build new skills in coding and embrace their innate creativity and curiosity.

(9) Alongside fostering development of soft skills (including a strong level of empathy) schools should seek opportunities to connect students with real-life work experiences.

Here is our summary of the skills and dispositions we abstracted from the executives' *expectations* statements. These statements may help *frame a school's curriculum* and highlight the *expected behaviors and skills* that students need to be taught, including:

- developing new technological skills;
- developing effective social and emotional skills;

- able to work in environments that will call for collaboration and teamwork;
- being cooperative and able to resolve workplace conflicts;
- learning how to learn and how to motivate others inclusiveness;
- being resilient enough to bounce back from adversity and hardship;
- practicing (a strong level of) empathy;
- being critical, creative, flexible, and innovative thinkers;
- being self-aware and self-regulatory;
- knowing "coding" tools and technologies;
- attending to their personal well-being;
- being able to communicate effectively through a host of mobile devices and digital platforms; and
- understand situations that disproportionately impact underserved communities.

What are *your expectations* for the students you teach? Our expectation (and hope) is that all P–12 students learn and practice these 3 Es: Always be *ethical, enthusiastic, and empathetic.*

What do you expect?

New and veteran teachers always begin a school year with *expectations* that may vary throughout the year.

Expectations that are clear, reasonable, consistent, enforced, encouraged, and well-communicated are at the "heart" of teaching and learning subject matter and character.

Your *expectations* probably began a week or two before school started. As *expected,* you used nonpaid time getting your classroom ready—arranging the desks, adding decorations, finding out if the equipment works, hanging posters, counting textbooks, and enjoying the quietness of preparation.

Most schools give students a choice on how to be greeted. By doing this, each student is empowered to choose how they want to be greeted. It can change daily. Students can choose between "high-fives, a fist bump, or a hug." The options are posted as a visual on the classroom door.

There is also an *expectation* that you to get to know your students names as soon as possible—that you review your classroom rules as soon as possible and that you post them.

Another *expectation* is that you "get to it," start teaching content, impress the students with your knowledge, and make it clear what you *expect* from them.

Most of your students' parents *expect* that you will send a letter or email to them during the first week of school in which you tell them how much you look forward to teaching their son/daughter this year.

The *expectation* rule: *stop thinking of what could go wrong and start thinking of what could go right.*

Your message board

Questions/Thoughts/Ideas

The Payoff

The most frequently asked question—the one we get most from educators and parents—*what's the payoff?*

One, a commitment to making character education an integral part of the education process will increase students' academic achievement.

For example, among middle-school students, the character strengths of perseverance, love, gratitude, hope, and perspective, predict academic achievement.

Two, character education in schools has a broad impact on students' pro-social and moral behaviors by developing their problem-solving skills, building positive peer relationships, enhancing their self-esteem, improving their interpersonal skills, and strengthening their ability at self-regulation (control).

A third "payoff"—an effective character education program shows that the school will become a more caring community, that discipline referrals will drop, that quality of peer and adult relationships will improve, and that students' will make a greater commitment to schooling and academic achievement.

All successful evaluation programs have a strong professional training component for teachers, counselors, administrators, parents, and community leaders.

Let's discuss the *benefits.*

Among middle-school students, the character strengths of perseverance, love, gratitude, hope, and perspective predict *academic achievement.* This is one very good reason for making a commitment to character education in classrooms and schools.

Research also tells us that the *culture of schools and the climate in classrooms* exert powerful influences on what students learn about authority, responsibility, justice, civility, and respect.

Character education programs that develop each student's problem-solving skills, enhances their self-esteem, improves their interpersonal skills, builds positive peer relationships, and strengthens their ability at self-regulation (control) has a major *impact on students' pro-social and moral behaviors.*

Very important benefits result when students are exposed in school, at home, in the community, and in their social media interactions to these *positive models of behavior:*

- Moral responsibility.
- Self-discipline.
- Respect for individual worth and human dignity.
- Public-spiritedness and the respect for law.
- Civility and the willingness to negotiate/compromise.

To know more

William H. Jeynes, "A Meta-Analysis on the Relationship Between Character Education and Student Achievement and Behavioral Outcomes," *Sage Journals*, Vol. 1, https://doi.org/10.1177/0013124517747681 (edited):

> *An extensive meta-analysis, including 52 studies, was undertaken on the relationship between character education and student achievement and behavioral outcomes. The results indicated that character education is associated with higher levels of educational outcomes, no matter what type of standardized or nonstandardized measure was*

> *employed. Character education was also related to higher levels of expressions of love, integrity, compassion, and self-discipline. Overall, character education had somewhat greater effects for children in high school rather than those who were in elementary school.*

"How Students Can Benefit from Character Education" *(https://www.teachnology.com/currenttrends/character_education/):*

Professors Berkowitz and Bier identified fifty-four character education programs backed by research. They found sixteen outcomes that most consistently and positively influenced students.

We have selected eight highest percentage outcomes:

- Sexual behavior (91 percent or ten of eleven studies);
- Character knowledge (87 percent);
- Social-moral cognition (74 percent);
- Problem-solving skills (64 percent);
- Emotional competency (64 percent);
- Relationships (62 percent);
- Attachment to school (61 percent); and
- Academic achievement (59 percent).

The Rand Corporation report notes that *a growing body of research indicates that social and emotional competencies, such as collaboration and self-management, have important roles in students' success, both in and out of school.*

Proficiency in these competencies can enhance academic achievement and attainment) improve students' attitudes and behaviors toward themselves and others, and have a positive impact on later-life outcomes, such as earnings (https://www.rand.org/content/dam/rand/pubs/research_reports/RR2700/RR2739/RAND_RR2739.pdf).

Our Q and A

To assist administrators, teachers, and others in schools, we offer nine questions along with the "payoff" for having an effective, dynamic character education program.

1. What is the environment/climate of the school and what should it be?

   Our answer is that at the very least it should be: safe, caring, civil, challenging, empowering.

2. What outcomes do school personnel, parents, and students desire for students who have attended the school for three or four years?

   Our answer is this question should be based on at least three categories: character, career, and citizenship.

3. What are the character traits/virtues that should permeate the curricula and co-curricula programs at the school?

   The answer to this question must be a list agreed upon by the school's stakeholders and incorporated into the mission of the school.

4. What thinking, communication, and social skills should permeate all subjects, programs, and instruction?

5. What special/intervention programs should be imple-
    mented to promote the character development of students,
    to enhance their social and emotional skills, and to foster
    their leadership and citizenship skills?

6. What must school personnel do to be sure that all school
    stakeholders are on the same page relative to the answers to
    the questions above?

7. What are the *expectations* for students regarding their
    behaviors?

8. What are the *expectations* regarding relationships at your
    school?

    - Students and students/students and parents/adult and
      students?
    - Teachers and parents/teachers and parents and admin-
      istrators? School and community?

9. How will school personnel (all stakeholders) know that
    their efforts to do the above have paid off?

    - How will programs and efforts be assessed?
    - How will students' academic, social, emotional, and char-
      acter behaviors and actions be assessed and evaluated?

Then we are always asked, *do character education initiatives
really work (pay off)?*

A national survey and report (character.org) described three
essential life-long skills that must be taught to children and young
adults.

1. Social skills and awareness (e.g., communi-
    cations skills, active listening, relationship
    skills, assertiveness, social awareness).

2. Personal improvement/Self-management and awareness (e.g., self-control, goal setting, relaxation techniques, self-awareness, emotional awareness).
3. Problem-solving/Decision-making.

The report states:

> *They found that schools that score higher on implementation of a variety of character education aspects also have higher state achievement scores. Most notably, such higher scores were most consistently and strongly related to the following four aspects of character education:*

1. *Parent and teacher modeling of character and promotion of character education.*
2. *Quality opportunities for students to engage in service activities.*
3. *Promoting a caring community and positive social relationships; and*
4. *Ensuring a clean and safe physical environment.*

Your message board

Questions/Thoughts/Ideas

About the Authors

Edward F. DeRoche, MA, MS, PhD was an elementary and middle school teacher and principal, a public school board member, a member of two private high school boards, a professor, program evaluator, student adviser, teacher trainer, and University of San Diego's School of Education dean.

Ed was a past president of the California Association of Teacher Educators and a member of the National Commission on Character Education. Currently, he is the Director of the Character Education Resource Center in the School of Leadership and Education Sciences at the University of San Diego.

He is a consultant, evaluator, author, teacher trainer, and a recipient of several awards including the "Sanford N. McDonald Award for Lifetime Achievement in Character Education" from character.org., the University of San Diego's School of Education's "Outstanding Administrator of the Year Award," and *The San Diego Union-Tribune's* "Educator of the Year Award."

Diane D. Johnson, BS (K–8), MA, known to many as Dee, has for the past thirty-one years been an integral part of teaching elementary and middle school in Connecticut.

She has been an active participant in the Best Training Mentor Program and the Anti-Bullying Harassment Committee. Dee was involved with the Connecticut Assets-Character Education, cochaired

South School Character Education, and headed up the KICS-Kids in Community Service program. As an adjunct professor, she taught two graduate classes focused on character education and multiple intelligences. She presented at the ASCD conference in Baltimore on multiple intelligences.

Dee also created and implemented a student council program for an elementary school. One rewarding experience was developing and participating in an inner city book collection for first graders.

With a teacher from the high school, they developed a writing mentor program. Each year, they would arrange time for the high school seniors and third-graders to write published poetry, nonfiction books, and fiction stories.

Many of the seniors and third-graders won writing awards statewide and nationally.

She managed to have time to get three masters and raise two children.